THE POSSIBILITIES of FULL SALVATION

Vic Reasoner

2120 Culverson Ave
Evansville, IN 47714-4811

© 2025 Victor Paul Reasoner
ISBN 979-8-9916819-2-6

THE POSSIBILITIES of FULL SALVATION

Humanity is divided into two groups: sinners and Christians. Sinners are unholy and Christians are holy. However, both groups can be divided into two additional categories. The purpose of this analysis is not to make things complicated; rather, the purpose is to understand how God's grace works in our lives. Grace can change our world. In order to find ourselves in this process we must begin with sin.

What is sin?

Sin is rebellion against God's law. God's existence is not open for debate. And implied in his existence is his authority. If he is God, then his rules are final. And since God has revealed himself through the holy writings we call the Scriptures or the Bible, what he says there becomes our final authority.

The good news is that God is not only sovereign but holy. We will look later at his holiness. For now we must begin with what he teaches about sin.

Because there are degrees and types of sin, the Scriptures give various definitions of sin. These definitions do not contradict each other, but they describe sin from different angles. These definitions also overlap.

- Sin is not believing in Christ (John 16:9)
- Sin is suppressing the truth (Rom 1:18)
- Sin is defiance against God's law (Rom 8:7)
- Sin is the opposite of faith (Rom 14:23)
- Sin is lawlessness (1 John 3:4)
- Sin is refusing to do good (Jas 4:17)

Our sinful acts are based on

- unbelief as the universal cause of all sin
- idolatry as the universal nature of all sin
- pride as the universal attitude of all sin
- self-will as the universal assertion of all sin
- love of the world which is in rebellion against God as the universal desire of all sin

The basic meaning of sin in the Old Testament is to miss or transgress an implied absolute standard of God. There are more terms in the Hebrew language of the Old Testament for sin than for goodness. We are a race of sinners. We are so proficient as sinners that an extensive vocabulary has developed to describe us. The New Testament contains twenty-eight synonyms for sin. The variations in meaning include: wrongdoing, unrighteousness, injustice, over-stepping, transgression, disobedience, failure to hear, carelessness, trespass, a false step, oversight, error, unintentional mistake, lawlessness, iniquity, godlessness, falling short, ignorance, a defect, loss, a fault, a crime, evil, wickedness, and unbelief.

As we begin to analyze these terms in Scripture we can see that

- sin is a condition and an act
- there are sins of commission and sins of omission
- there are unintentional and deliberate sins

Although unintentional sin does not stem from rebellion, ignorance is no excuse. We can still cause great damage even if we did not deliberately choose to break the law.

Everyone has broken God's law. In God's mercy he has provided his Son as the substitute who has received the penalty for all our sins. Until now we have been focused on deliberate acts of sin. Yet the Scripture also makes it clear that we commit acts of sin because we are sinful. And so we also need to look at our sinful nature.

Two types of sin

While acts of willful sin are acts of rebellion, they stem from a sinful nature. Our sinful nature is the abiding result of Adam's original act of sin. Since he was our father, we have universally inherited that same likeness. We are corrupt. God did not create us in this condition, but our corruption is the tragic result which has prevailed ever since Adam and Eve opened the door to sin.

Apart from grace, every inclination of the thoughts of our heart is only evil all the time (Gen 6:5). We have all turned aside and become corrupt. There is no one who does good, not even one (Ps 14:2-3, 53:3). We are sinful from the moment of conception (Ps 51:5). The wicked are estranged from the womb; they go astray from birth (Ps 58:3). The heart is deceitful above all things (Jer 17:9). Jesus said we are evil (Matt

7:11; Luke 11:13).

We are all under sin (Rom 3:9). There is not even one who is righteous (Rom 3:10-18; Ps 143:2). We are dead in transgressions and sins, gratifying the cravings of our sinful nature (Eph 2:1-3). Our old self is corrupt through deceitful desires (Eph 4:22). We are helpless (Rom 5:6). We are sold as a slave to sin (Rom 7:14). We are subject to "the law of sin and death" (Rom 8:2). The flesh is at war with God (Rom 8:7).

We have a sinful nature (Rom 8:8). We quarrel and fight, covet and murder because we have passions warring within (Jas 4:1-2). Sinful desire is the corruption that is in the world (2 Pet 1:4). All have sinned (Rom 3:23) because all are sinners. Sinful actions proceed from a sinful heart (Mark 7:21-22). Anyone who claims to be without a sinful nature is thus deceived and the truth is not in him (1 John 1:8). The sinner is:

- energized by Satan (Eph 2:1-2)
- blinded by Satan (2 Cor 4:3-4)
- controlled by Satan (1 John 5:19)

To say that we are totally corrupt does not mean that we are all equally as bad as we can possibly become. Total corruption means that every aspect of our personality has been corrupted by sin. "The whole head is sick" (Isa 1:5), including our understanding, imagination, memory, reason, will, conscience, and affections.

- Our intellect is darkened. We do not think clearly. In fact, the choice to sin is moral insanity. Our

understanding, imagination, memory, and reason are faulty.
- Our will is perverted. We want what is bad for us and run from that which is good for us. Thus, we are bound by sinful desires and habits.
- Our emotions are alienated. We are afraid of God and love sin. Even our conscience is not trustworthy.

The result is that we are totally helpless to save ourselves from this blight of sin. Religion does not help. We are turned in on ourselves and away from God.

Two types of sinners

The sinner who is asleep

However, the sinner who is asleep does not care. The Bible describes the sinner as *dead* toward God and as *asleep* concerning his or her own condition. Sinners who are asleep are good at justifying themselves. Some people even brag about particular sins at which they are especially proficient. They find comfort in doubting or even denying God's existence. Like a child playing near a cliff, the fact that we are unaware of our danger does not make our situation any less dangerous.

The awakened sinner

When we are unable to change, and even uninterested in changing, God in his grace makes the first move in waking us up. In his love he begins drawing us to himself. We do not ask for these overtures, but God awakens us anyway.

Sometimes it is through a crisis — even affliction, a song, or a Christian's witness that we begin to think seriously about our life. Each person's story is unique. Usually, however, it comes through the preaching of God's law.

- The law defines sin (Rom 7:7).
- The law convicts of sin (Gal 3:19). This is the ordinary means through which sinners are convicted.
- The law even provokes sin (Rom 7:7-8).
- The law drives us to Christ who alone can save us (Gal 3:24).

The one thing the law cannot do, however, is save the sinner. According to Galatians 3:21, the law cannot impart life. Yet it is indispensable as a diagnostic tool. It is like a mirror which reveals our flaws but cannot remove them.

The work of the Holy Spirit convinces us of our guilt and warns us of our sin, our unrighteousness, and the coming judgment (John 16:8-11). God temporarily restores our conscience, our awareness of him, and the consciousness that we have broken his law. Our mind is illuminated, our will is strengthened, and our senses are heightened.

Preliminary grace is the God-given desire to please God and obey his law (Rom 7:16, 22). The preaching of the gospel enables anyone to believe (Rom 10:8-21). Paul explained that his preaching was accompanied by the power of the Holy Spirit (1 Cor 2:4; 1 Thess 1:5).

The power of the gospel comes from God (2 Cor 3:5). That grace is able to bring to life those who are spiritually dead (Eph 2:1-8). The gift of God is faith, grace, and salvation. Salvation is *all* of grace, beginning with the moment the sleeper is awakened (Eph 5:14).

According to John 12:32 all men are drawn to Christ. This gracious drawing is resistible, but it provides everyone with the opportunity to believe. Yet that preliminary grace may be thwarted (2 Cor 6:1-2; Gal 2:21; Heb 10:29).

This preliminary light appears to everyone to a greater or lesser degree. Most people, however, stifle it and then forget that they ever had such an experience. Others try to save themselves by resolving to try harder and do better. Before his conversion, the apostle Paul described his struggle as an awakened sinner. Intellectually, he approved of living right, but the harder he tried to do right the more he discovered that he also wanted to do wrong. He felt miserable, but wrong eventually trumped right.

Jesus taught in John 15:5 that apart from him we can do nothing. Therefore, God must initiate the process of salvation and enable us to respond.

After Peter's sermon at Pentecost, his hearers were cut to the heart and asked, "What shall we do?" (Acts 2:37; see also Acts 16:30). According to Acts 5:31, God enables repentance. In Acts 8:14-17, the Samaritans had accepted the Word of God and had been baptized, but they had not received the Holy Spirit. Yet the Holy Spirit was already at work in their lives.

In Acts 8:26-40 we see the Ethiopian eunuch was moved by the Spirit to read Isaiah and Philip was led to join him in the Bible study.

Paul was also under preliminary grace for three days until he received the Holy Spirit (Acts 9:4-18, 22:16). Cornelius feared and obeyed God before he was born again, but he was given repentance unto life (Acts 10:35,11:18). After Paul and Barnabas left the Jewish synagogue, they urged the congregation to continue in the grace of God (Acts 13:43). Yet they were not yet born again. The text describes an operation of divine grace working in their hearts while they were hearing the gospel.

Lydia's heart was opened to the gospel and she became a believer (Acts 16:14-16). She was faithful to the grace she had received, so God gave her more grace. Regarding both the travelers on the Emmasus Road and Lydia, Oden explained, "Their eyes became open not because they sought God, but because God sought them (John 9; Acts 9:18)."

Romans 2:4 teaches that God continues to lead sinners to repentance. Verse 14 describes the work of conscience within pagans who do not have the Scriptures. Romans 5:16-18 teaches that the gracious gift came to all who sinned. However, everyone is not saved. The gracious gift, then, is this preliminary grace.

The transformation of a nonchalant sinner who does not care, into a troubled sinner who is beside himself with concern, is so great that often it is assumed they are converted. They may even be baptized and join the church, but they are not yet a Christian. Nominal Christians presume they are saved because of a decision, a declaration, a ritual, or their good works. A true Christian has received the Holy Spirit who makes him or her holy.

What is holiness?

God is awesome and glorious. He is unimpeachable. He is separate from and above all that is sinful. He is absolutely perfect and pure. It is this holiness which distinguishes him from everything else. His law is an expression of his holiness. His anger is his holy response to sin. Even his jealousy is a holy resistance to any attempt to share his glory. But the good news is that his love is also an expression of his holiness. His love compels him to take the initiative and make the initial overture of grace to us. But he cannot fellowship with us in our rotten condition. Therefore, he commands us to be holy *as* he is holy. We cannot be as holy as he is because he is the source of all our holiness. But we can be made like him, we can be restored to our original state, through his grace.

Grace is not forbearance but enablement. If I cannot pay my insurance premium on time, the company may extend to me a grace period. But if I am still completely unable to pay it at the end of the grace period, I am no better off. The love of God leads him to satisfy our sin debt on our behalf, while at the same time maintaining his integrity and righteousness. But his love does not stop with reconciling a relationship which we broke through sin. He begins the process of restoration and transformation, making us like himself. He does this by giving us his Spirit. It is the Holy Spirit living within us who makes us a true Christian.

Two levels of Christians

To pass from death to life is the greatest event that will ever happen to us. While it is possible to make the Christian life too high, the practical reality is that it is almost taught at too low a level.

I do not want to perpetuate some kind of Christian caste system which delineates between ordinary and super-Christians. But there is growth and that development does not all come at once. The apostle John described the church to which he was writing. He called some of them little children, some of them young men, and some of them fathers. They are all God's children, but they are not all at the same level of maturity.

All true Christians are forgiven for their past sins. All true Christians have the Holy Spirit living in them. In the book of Acts the terms *baptized* (1:5), *come upon* (1:8), *filled* (2:4), and *receiving the gift of the Holy Spirit* (2:38), all refer to the same event and that event is regeneration. Biblical writers refer to the giving of the Holy Spirit as being filled, being baptized, being endued with power. The Spirit was sent, given, poured out, and fell. These terms are synonymous and cannot be used to make artificial distinctions. Luke used seven different phrases a total of twenty-three times in Luke and Acts to describe the coming of the Spirit, and they are merely different aspects of the same operation.

The Holy Spirit gives Christians victory over intentional sin. Christians are not "sinners saved by grace." They are holy. The New Testament calls them *saints*. That word literally means *holy ones*. In thirty-eight New Testament passages where the Christian is described, they are never referred to as *sinners*.

They have been set apart from their old identity as sinners. They have been forgiven for all past sins. They have been delivered from the penalty of sin. The power and bondage of sin has been broken. It is still possible for them to commit sin, but for the first time it is now possible for them *not* to sin. The Spirit also gives them assurance that they have been adopted into God's family. But there is a difference.

The baby Christian

Twice the Bible uses the term *born again* (1 Pet 1:3, 23). We are born of God (1 John 5:1). We are born from above (John 3:3, 7). We are born of water and the Spirit (John 3:5).

The young Christian has been born again or born from above. We are made alive (Eph 2:5). Regeneration is spiritual resurrection (John 5:25; Eph 2:1). It is new creation (2 Cor 5:17). We are created in Christ Jesus (Eph 2:10) and we are washed (Titus 3:5),

All of these glorious gifts are a present reality through the administration of the Holy Spirit. But the new Christian still has the old nature of sin. God reigns in their lives, but the blight of sin remains. Unattended, it can steal their peace and trip them up. They must learn how to detect it and how to constantly say "No" to it. It can play like it is dead and then come back to life, attempting to overpower us. We may be dead to sin so long as we understand sin is not dead to us. We are still liable to temptation.

Paul explained to the Galatians that now the struggle is between the sinful desires of that old nature and the Holy Spirit who is in control. He keeps us from doing what we would have done before as a sinner, but if we do not walk in the power of the Spirit it is possible for us to disregard his warnings and deliberately choose what is wrong. Is there a better way? All Christians are holy, but that holiness may be perfected (2 Cor 7:1).

The adult Christian

The gradual or *progressive* work of *sanctification* is the work of the Spirit beginning with preliminary grace and continuing until final glorification. Christ continually purges everyone who is abiding in him (John 15:2). Discipleship is essentially progressive sanctification. In its broadest sense discipleship is the metaphor most descriptive of the doctrine of progressive sanctification.

God will never strip from us our ability to choose, but he can cleanse us from this old sinful nature which attempts to sabotage us. This cleansing was also provided through the price Christ paid for us on the cross. While it does not necessarily happen the same way in every person, the Holy Spirit will reveal to us what is really happening in our mind and will somehow bring this problem to a head. All we can do is acknowledge it and trust him to deliver us from it.

Scripture is pessimistic about our sinful nature, but optimistic about God's grace. "He who calls us is faithful and will do it" (1 Thess 5:24). God can save completely or to the uttermost (Heb 7:25). This Greek phrase *eis to panteles* means salvation is to the farthest extent, to the greatest degree, to the most distant point.

Full salvation is not only freedom from the guilt, the bondage, and the power of sin, but cleansing from the pollution and nature of sin and ultimately deliverance from the very presence of sin.

How much of this complete salvation may be experienced in this life? "Now to him who is able to do immeasurably more than all we ask or imagine, according to his power that is at work with us" (Eph 3:20). If God is sovereign, there is no limit to the grace he can extend. But it is not helpful to create a series of easy steps which every seeker must follow. While God desires the same relationship with each of us, the path we follow is not always the same. Sanctification is messy business.

We surrender to the lordship of Christ when we are born again. However, we do not really know at that time what God's will may involve. There may be many points in time in which we accept the will of God as it unfolds. When we yield ourselves without reservation, he sanctifies us without reservation. There could be several crisis points in which this happens. Ultimately, God will fill us so full of his love, that everything that is not consistent with his love will be displaced. As we continue to walk in the Spirit at this higher level we can live consistently as a mature Christian. The Bible uses more than one motif for the holy life — maturity, inner healing, cleansing, restoration, realignment, circumcision, perfect love, entire sanctification, and covenant relationship.

Entire sanctification is the condition of loving God with all our heart. This love expels all sin, cleansing the heart from all unrighteousness. This term corresponds with the term *Christian perfection* or *maturity*, but neither term implies the end of growth or progress.

The Problem of Perfection

Christ commands us to be perfect. How is this possible? As far back as the Greek philosophers, there have been two definitions of perfection. While Plato had concluded that only God was perfect, Aristotle defined perfection as that which accomplishes the purpose for which it was created. Thus, Plato viewed perfection in the absolute sense while Aristotle's concept was applied by Methodist theologians to mean that Christian perfection was to love God with our whole being and our neighbor as ourselves.

We continue to use this word in both senses. The Latin word *perfectus* means unimprovable. This was a static concept. But the Greek word *teleios* means completeness or fulfillment, total commitment without reservation. This is a dynamic concept. Jesus does not command us to be *as* perfect as God. John Wesley explained that our perfection is in kind though not in degree. Our perfection is a relative perfection. When we are filled with the love of God, God imputes perfection to us. Yet we lack knowledge. We make mistakes. We struggle with infirmities. The best of us still need the intercession of Christ to atone for our omissions, shortcomings, mistakes in judgment and practice, and all our defects.

Holy living begins with the baptism of the Holy Spirit when we are born again. Christian Perfection is a relative perfection in which the babe in Christ reaches his full stature, being conformed to the image of Christ. The sanctifying grace of the Holy Spirit imparted to us can so fill us with the love of God that while we are thus filled, everything contrary to that love is displaced. When we love God with our whole being, God imputes perfection to us, meaning that we are fulfilling his purpose for us.

The Promise of God

This *full* salvation is promised in Scripture. "The reason the Son of God appeared was to destroy the works of the devil" (1 John 3:8). "Christ loved the church and gave himself up for her, that he might sanctify her, having cleansed her by the washing of water with the word, so that he might present the church to himself in splendor, without spot or wrinkle or any such thing, that she might be holy and without blemish" (Eph. 5:25-27). "By sending his own Son in the likeness of sinful flesh and for sin, he condemned sin in the flesh, in order that the righteous requirement of the law might be fulfilled in us, who walk not according to the flesh but according to the Spirit" (Rom 8:3-4). "He has given us his very great and precious promises, so that through them you may participate in the divine nature and escape the corruption in the world caused by evil desires" (2 Pet 1:4).

1 John 1:9 encompasses entire sanctification as well as justification. When we confess our sins, God is faithful to forgive us. When we receive a deeper revelation of our sinful nature and confess that, God is also faithful to cleanse us from all iniquity.

The Command of God

This *full* salvation is commanded. "Walk before me and be perfect" (Gen 17:1). "Serve him with a perfect heart and a willing mind" (1 Chr 28:9). "You therefore must be perfect, as your heavenly Father is perfect" (Matt 5:48). The perfection or completeness commanded is explained in v 43 where Jesus said we are to love even our enemies. Thus the context prior to v 48 is dealing with perfect love and v 48 is a concluding statement which begins with the connecting word *therefore*.

"You shall love the Lord your God with all your heart and with all your soul and with all your mind" (Matt 22:37; Mark 12:30). Paul commanded the Corinthian believers to "be perfect" (2 Cor 13:11). "You shall be holy, for I am holy" (1 Pet 1:16).

In addition to the imperatives just cited, a second class of texts could be categorized as exhortations: "I urge you to present your bodies a living sacrifice, holy, acceptable to God" (Rom 12:1). Under the old covenant worship involved offering sacrifices to God. There were burnt offerings, grain or meat offerings, peace offerings, guilt or sin offerings. Normally animals were put to death. This symbolized substitution as human guilt was transferred to the animal sacrifice. By the time of the temple in Jerusalem, so much blood was spilled into the drainage system that the brook Kidron, into which it dumped, ran red.

Then Christ came and became our sacrifice, doing away with animal sacrifices. The worship of the church in Rome, with its breaking of the bread and sharing of the communion cup, must have appeared strange to the

Jews, because there were no animal sacrifices, and to the Romans because there were no sacrifices offered to Caesar. Although God took the blood out of sacrifice, he did not take the sacrifice out of worship. Now he calls on us to present ourselves as *living* sacrifices. God wants us to live for him as a freed servant (see Exod 21:2-11), not necessarily to die for him.

Prayers for *Full* Salvation

Our *full* salvation is prayed for. In his high priestly prayer, Jesus prayed,

> Sanctify them in the truth; your word is truth. As you sent me into the world, I have sent them into the world. For them I sanctify myself, that they too may be truly sanctified. I do not ask for these only, but also for those who will believe in me through their word, that they may all be one, just as you, Father, are in me, and I in you, that they also may be in us, so that the world may believe that you have sent me. The glory that you have given me I have given to them, that they may be one even as we are one, I in them and you in me, that they may become perfected in one (John 17:17-23).

This verse is not necessarily proof that the disciples were initially or entirely sanctified at that point in time. Nor does the sanctification of the Savior refer specifically to the categories of initial or entire sanctification. However, all this is potentially included when the prayer is expanded to include all who will believe.

The result of his atoning sacrifice is that the sanctification, both initial and entire, now provided, produces in us deliverance through the Word, unity within the body of Christ, access into the presence of God, a reflection of the nature of God, and credibility within the world. Ironically, the Holy Spirit is not mentioned in John 17, but his sanctifying work may be implied from chapters 14-16.

Most of Paul's letters contain prayers for Christian perfection. They are typically addressed to the saints or literally to the holy ones. They are initially sanctified, but not entirely. However, there are no such prayers in the pastoral letters. The significance may be that Timothy and Titus were already mature believers.

In 2 Corinthians 13:9-11 Paul declared, "Our prayer is for your perfection." This is a prayer for restoration and wholeness. This includes a restoration of order in the Corinthian church, as well as the recovery of moral purity. Originally this word *perfection* was used for setting dislocated bones. The meaning is to mend, restore, or perfect. Even after we are born again, there are areas of our personality that are out of alignment and need to be relocated.

In Ephesians 1:15-23 Paul prays that God would give the saints in Ephesus the Spirit of wisdom and revelation so that they may know him better. The Spirit inspired the revelation of the mind of God through Scripture, but he is also in every believer revealing Christ as a personal Savior.

The believer has already received the seal of the Spirit (v 13), an internal assurance of acceptance which no mere rational assent could bring. Yet there is more to behold: the hope of his calling, the riches of our glorious inheritance, and the might of the divine power made available to us.

We are called to experience the treasury of blessings for the people of God in time and in eternity. Paul resumes this prayer in Ephesians 3:14-21, praying that we might become mighty through the Spirit (v 16). Not only does Paul pray for a supernatural empowerment, in v 17 Paul prays that Christ may dwell in our hearts through faith. While the Spirit of Christ indwells all believers, here Paul uses a compound word meaning to settle down or to make a home in your hearts. The Spirit makes himself at home in the sense that we become rooted and grounded in love. When we are justified by faith, the love of God is poured out into our hearts (Rom 5:5). Now Paul prays that we might become established in love. In this deeper relationship, we are enabled to realize the magnitude of God's love — how wide, how long, how high, and how deep. As our spiritual capacity increases, we can receive a fuller measure of the Holy Spirit.

While all true Christians have the Spirit, Daniel Steele explained, "The vessel is too weak and too small to contain all that God desires to pour into it. It must be enlarged and strengthened."

To be filled with God is to be emptied of self. John Wesley commented that this describes "a perfection far beyond a bare freedom from sin." While we can never contain the fullness of God, we can be filled unto the full measure of blessing and maturity God has for us.

In Philippians 1:4-6, Paul prays that the Spirit will carry his ongoing work in us unto completion or perfection. According to verses 9-11 this would produce

- a love growing in knowledge of the truth and discernment which is able to react properly in every crisis
- an ability to discern the more excellent way. Love functions as an internal monitor.
- a purity of character that reflects sincerity (simplicity of motive) and is not offensive
- a fullness of the fruit of righteousness. All Christians have an imputed righteousness that comes through faith in Christ (Phil 3:9), but here Paul describes a condition of being full of this righteousness. Wesley observed, "Here also the apostle is far from speaking of justification only."

In Philippians 3:10-11 Paul himself longs to know Christ better. While Christ suffered and died, then was resurrected, the order for the Christian is reversed. First he is raised from spiritual death. Thus, we first know God in the power of Christ's resurrection.

Then we come to know Christ through the fellowship of his sufferings. The only suffering which becomes a means of grace is suffering which causes us to look away from ourselves and focus upon his passion. Although Christ suffered alone, we need not ever suffer alone. We were not present historically when Christ suffered on the cross, but our suffering can connect with his.

The third level of intimacy with God is through death. This seems like a paradox, but it is a deeper death to self-centeredness. It is the death of what remains of the old life.

Martin Luther frequently described sin as the heart turned in upon itself. This sinful propensity remains after the new birth. Many who profess to be Christians are not truly Christian, yet it seems that most who are Christians are still interested in very little beyond themselves. Paul complained that everyone looks out for his own interests (Phil 2:21). But perfect love is not self-seeking (1 Cor 13:5). Jesus taught us to seek first his kingdom (Matt 6:33), but few Christians do. The perfecting grace of God turns the heart outward.

Thus, entire sanctification is a spiritual death. It is a more perfect conformity to the nature of Christ. Just as Paul distinguished between Christian perfection and bodily perfection in Philippians 3:12,15, so he distinguished between a conformity to the image of Christ in v 10 and the future change of our physical bodies in v 21.

In Colossians 1:9-14, Paul continued to pray that they would have a growing knowledge of God's will which would result in a practical conformity with that will in three areas:

- more fruit — the holiness of the regenerate life is the fruit of a tree of life within as well as his own habits and acts. But the fruitfulness of the Christian life knows no limits. As our knowledge of God's will grows the fruits of obedience will also grow.
- a greater power in our lives producing more strength, endurance, patience, and joy
- thankfulness — gratitude for the benefits of redemption

Yet we are not to be passive in this process. Paul said he labored, struggling with all the energy he could muster, counseling and teaching so that every person might be presented perfect in Christ (1:28-29).

To be *filled with knowledge* in Colossians 1:9 means to be fully assured. In Colossians 2:2 Paul expressed his desire that they might know the freedom of mind and confidence that comes from a full understanding of the mystery of God in Christ. The full assurance of understanding includes a systematic grasp of all the truths and treasures of the faith. It is the realization that all truth is united in the person of Christ (v 3). It was their safeguard against the deceitfulness of empty philosophy (2:8), as well as the emerging gnosticism and later forms of scepticism.

This full assurance of understanding is an abiding and continual affirming by the Spirit of truth which produces a life of confidence. The result is that we are no longer infants, tossed back and forth by the waves, and blown here and there by every wind of teaching (Eph 4:14).

Church leaders are to be mature Christians who hold the deep truths of the faith with a pure conscience (1 Tim 3:9). We can know we are of the truth (1 John 3:19). It is an anointing from Christ which confirms truth and discerns error (1 John 2:20,27, 4:6). It is an understanding which reveals the truth about Christ (1 John 5:20).

In Colossians 4:12 a colleague of Paul also prays earnestly for two things — that we may stand perfect or complete *and* fully assured, having a greater sense of God's presence and acceptance.

In the first letter written to the church at

Thessalonica we read that they are in God the Father and in the Lord Jesus Christ (1:1). If any man be in Christ, he is a new creation (2 Cor 5:17). According to v 4 they are brethren, elect by God. In 4:8 we also discover that they have the Holy Spirit. God is giving them (present tense) the Spirit. And he came in much assurance (1:5). He also gave them joy (1:6).

According to 1 Thessalonians 1:3, their faith produced good works; their love prompted labor, and their hope inspired endurance. According to 1:7 they were a model or pattern. Verse 8 records their witness was like a trumpet blast that covered all of Macedonia. They had turned from idols to serve the living and true God and the news of their conversion had covered their whole region.

Timothy had returned to Paul bringing a good report (1 Thess 3:6) about their faith and love. In 4:9 Paul acknowledged that he had no need to instruct them about brotherly love. Therefore, it might come as a surprise that Paul states in 3:10 "night and day we pray most earnestly." Paul said he is praying super-excessively that what is lacking in their faith might be perfected. The verb *perfect* means to put in right order or restore to its former condition. It is a medical term.

They needed an increase in love (1 Thess 3:12). Paul prays for the enlargement of their souls. The word *increase* signifies the growth of the soul in the sphere of love, and the word *abound* signifies the outward manifestation of that love. Thus, Paul has utilized two words which defy restriction.

According to 1 Thessalonians 1:3 their labor was prompted by their love. They had love, but they needed more love. God's love can flow from us only when he continually flows into us. God wants to increase our intake and our outflow. Sometimes, however, it seems the demand is greater than the supply. But God can enlarge our capacity to love each other and to love everyone. Paul seems to indicate in the last part of v 12 that he has that kind of love for them. And he is praying that they will also have that kind of love.

They also needed more stability (1 Thess 3:13). It is God's plan to so cleanse the church that they are holy and blameless (Eph 5:27). Paul testified in 1 Thessalonians 2:10 that he had lived holy, righteous, and blameless among them. Now he is praying that they may be established blameless in holiness (3:13); and again in 5:23 he prays that their spirit, soul, and body be kept blameless.

This blamelessness portrays what perfect Christians should be. To be holy is to be morally blameless. In this life we will never know freedom from ignorance, mistake, temptation, or a thousand infirmities, but we can be blameless. Our motives can be pure.

Part of what it means to be blameless is stated in Philippians 2:14, "Do everything without complaining or arguing so that you may become blameless and pure." According to Colossians 3:13-14, if any man have a complaint, we are to bear with each other, forgive each other [not cast blame], and above all put on love, which binds them all together in perfect unity.

God can deliver from a complaining spirit. In Ephesians 5:27 Paul says he can cleanse us — that is the negative side. First Thessalonians 3:12-13 is the positive answer — he strengthens, establishes, reinforces, and braces in holiness. This results in an increase and overflow of love.

The Thessalonians already had some holiness, but it needed reinforcement. God can provide extra bracing to stabilize us. Notice this stabilization is not provided at the moment of death nor by the return of Christ. Paul's prayer was that they would be found blameless and holy *when* the Lord Jesus appeared. This appearing of Christ will then confirm us in a permanent state of holiness which implies the end of probation.

They needed a completion of sanctification. They were already initially sanctified. In 1 Thessalonians 4:3 Paul teaches that their sanctification was God's will. Paul says it is God's will that they should keep on abstaining from these sexual sins. Thus, they were already partially sanctified and separate from sexual impurity. So were the Corinthians. Paul wrote that some of them were involved in sexual sins, "but you were washed, you were sanctified, you were justified" (1 Cor 6:11). This is initial sanctification which comes along with justification. God calls all believers to live such a holy life (1 Thess 4:7).

But 1 Thessalonians 5:23 this is more than a good-luck wish, it is the desire of the Spirit that our sanctification or holiness be entire. This word means all, whole, or entirely and is coupled with a second word which means to perfect. It speaks strongly of a completeness to sanctification. The second word *entire* means complete, sound in every part. Paul prays that something will happen to us which will make us complete. Since the verb is *sanctify*, the focus of the prayer is that we are sanctified completely.

Paul prays that they would attain the goal completely. This prayer was expressed for those who had experienced the grace of God. Paul said in 1

Thessalonians 3:10 that he prayed earnestly night and day that God would supply what was lacking in their faith. He prays for sanctifying grace that reaches the whole life and the whole person. All believers are cleansed as they walk in light, so that their mistakes and shortcomings are not imputed against them; but this is a deeper cleansing which leaves nothing out, penetrating body, soul, spirit, and cleansing through and through, entirely and completely.

It cannot be assumed that Paul is praying for the wholeness of the Thessalonian church since he referred in his prayer to the components of individual human personality. While the Savior prayed for the unity of his spiritual body in John 17, here Paul prays for the individuals comprising that body that this entire sanctification will pervade their whole being. What will this entire sanctification do? First Thessalonians 5:12-22 imply at least nine graces:

- It will give us a respect for spiritual authority and for preaching (v 20)
- It will help us live in peace with one another (v 13b)
- It will give us a sensitivity to spiritual needs. The lazy need to be admonished, the fearful need to be encouraged, the weak need to be propped up — it will take patience to deal with them all (v 14).
- It will deliver us from a vindictive, get-even spirit (v 15) and make us kind.
- It will make us joyful and deliver us from blaming and grumbling (v 16)
- It will make our prayer life more consistent (v 17)
- It will make us more thankful; thankful in all cir-

cumstances (v 18). Actually vv 16-18 describes unbroken praise to God, unbroken communion with God, and unbroken awareness of God.
- It will make us more obedient to the Spirit and more discerning of the Spirit (vv 19, 21)
- It will help us live more consistently and avoid every evil and questionable practice (v 22)

Then Paul prayed that this condition be maintained in them until the return of Christ. According to 1 Thessalonians 5:24, the one who calls you is faithful and he will do it, not simply impute it.

John Wesley said no man can live higher than this, but no man need to live short of this. "Now to him who is able to do immeasurably more than all we ask or imagine, according to his power that is at work within us" (Eph 3:20). The process has already begun. The Holy Spirit is already at work. And so with Charles Wesley we sing,

> Finish then thy new creation,
> Pure and spotless let us be;
> Let us see thy great salvation
> Perfectly restored in thee;
> Changed from glory into glory,
> Till in heaven we take our place,
> Till we cast our crowns before thee,
> Lost in wonder, love, and praise.

In 2 Thessalonians 1:11-12 Paul prayed that the church, who were called out of sin and called unto holiness, be deemed worthy of this calling and thus be glorified by the grace that counts them and makes them worthy. Paul's prayer is for an inward perfection of goodness and an outward perfection of faithfulness and consistency. Finally Paul carries us forward in his prayer to the day when this worthiness shall be acknowledged to be complete "on the day he comes to be glorified in his holy people" (v 10). "What they shall be he will have made them" is the meaning of the last phrase in Paul's prayer.

In 2 Thessalonians 2 Paul again prays. He prays in vv 16-17 that the Thessalonian Christians be consoled and established. Through the love and grace of God they have already experienced everlasting comfort and good hope. *Good hope* describes that part of the everlasting gift which has reference to the future. Paul prayed that the Lord himself, in unity with the Father, console their inner man by the word that invigorates and keeps their outer life steadfast in every good work and in every good doctrine.

While they had already received eternal encouragement, Paul is concerned that they not become quickly unsettled or alarmed (2 Thess 2:2). Therefore he prays that their hearts will be kept strong in this same consolation and their life established in obedience. The consistency of a full obedience, implied by *every* good word and deed, depends on the establishment of a firm faith in the Christian doctrine (2 Thess 2:15). The life that a Christian should desire is a life of entire goodness based upon perfect truth. In 3:3 Paul declares that the Lord is faithful and will establish us.

In 2 Thessalonians 3, Paul has been requesting prayer for himself when he breaks out in prayer for them at v 5. Paul prays for their direction into the love of God and into the patience of Christ. "In the strength of the love of God, always poured abundantly upon and around, and into the soul, there is no duty past performance, and no difficulty that may not be overcome. No higher prayer can be offered to God than this, that by the sweet influence of His Spirit we may be drawn from every lower affection, released from every base impediment, and have our entire being and all that is in it thrown open to the unhindered operation of the love of God." Then Paul literally prays for the steadfastness of patience that is Christ's. This will result in the steadfast obedience described in v 4. The specific meaning of this prayer is that it may please the Lord to remove every hindrance to our perfect union and harmony with our Lord in his example of endurance unto death.

At 2 Thessalonians 3:16 Paul returns to conclude his prayer. He prays that the Savior himself administer the blessings of his peace. That peace abides on the entire assembly through the abiding presence of the Lord. He can give us peace at all times and in all circumstances. The result is that we may expect a permanent, uninterrupted assurance of his acceptance. This peace of Christ incorporates all that is included in perfect spiritual prosperity. Yet this bold petition also demands that the rage of Satan and the wrath of men should not only praise God, but be turned to the deeper joy of his servant. The previous verses teach the Thessalonians to expect that the unrest and disorder of evil men should result in a far more exceeding peace for the devout. The voice of the Lord may not always hush the storm around or within the soul, but always and by all means he will give his peace in that inner man which ought never to be penetrated by anxiety.

In Hebrews 13:20-21, the writer prays, "May God equip you with everything good for doing his will." Here the verb *equip* is one of the New Testament words for perfection. This perfection "signifies the entire deliverance of the soul from everything that would hinder the complete performance of the will of God." The God of holiness is petitioned to do his own good pleasure within us so that we are able to manifest his good pleasure externally. He works internally, conforming us to his own image; and thus we are enabled to do every good work.

Finally, Peter prays, "And the God of all peace, who called you to his eternal glory in Christ, after you have suffered a little while, will himself restore you and make you strong, firm and steadfast. To him be the power for ever and ever. Amen" (1 Pet 5:10-11).

Here the emphasis is not upon suffering, but upon grace. Suffering demonstrates our need for growth in grace. Although Peter's emphasis in this first letter is that Christians will suffer (see 1:6) and that trials should not take us by surprise (4:12), persecution and stress, trials and afflictions do not sanctify — they reveal to what degree we are sanctified.

There are four synonyms, all future tense verbs, in 1 Peter 5:10 which are a promise of what God's grace can do in us between now and the end. He can *restore*. He can *establish*. Peter says the grace of God will confirm and support us. The word is used in v 9 where it tells us to stand firm in the faith. We have an invisible means of support. God has the grace to help us stand firm; make you hard, firm, solid. In Acts 14:22 Paul and Barnabas strengthened the disciples and encouraged them to remain true. They preached that we must go through many hardships to enter the kingdom of God. The kingdom is both now and later. We enter the kingdom now through the new birth; we enter heaven later by remaining true. We need this establishing grace so that we will persevere. Paul ends Romans with this same word: "Now to him who is able to establish you by my gospel" (Rom 16:25).

He can *strengthen*. Grace will keep us from collapsing. He will *settle*. He will establish us on a firm foundation. Grace will prevent you from being swept away. We can have solid support *around* us and a secure foundation *under* us. Every true Christian hungers for these dynamics, but some theologies offer little encouragement.

How did *full salvation* get so complicated?

If the Holy Scriptures are so full of this *full salvation*, why is there so much confusion, discord, and doctrinal wrangling on the subject? My master's thesis, my doctoral dissertation, as well as post-doctoral research, has been devoted to this topic. My research attempts to cover the topic across two thousand years of church history and by interacting with about twenty different positions. That work is available for documentation and is a reference point for many statements from primary sources (see the last page for information). I will not repeat that methodology here. Instead, I want to provide an answer that will help you cut through the confusion and understand God's will for your life.

The whole church everywhere has always taught that Christians are in some sense holy. And some form of Christian perfection has been held in every age. Testimonies might be gathered from every period. Yet in different periods of time and among different movements often a part has been taught as the whole. God has always had a people and his people have always been holy, but at different periods in church history there have been different emphases on the holy life. While some differences are substantive, others are more a matter of accent and we can learn something from each emphasis. Ephesians 3:10 speaks of the manifold wisdom of God. This word *manifold* has been translated as *many-sided* or *variegated*. Just as a diamond refracts light from many angles, so the church has emphasized Christian holiness from many vantage points. Yet there has always been a corresponding danger that we substitute a partial understanding for the bigger picture.

- In the earliest days of Christianity persecution and even martyrdom had to be accepted as a consequence of faith. Sainthood was then conveyed to those who had suffered for the faith. While persecution is still the case today in some parts of the world, where the external threat has subsided, the way to holiness became harsh — with seekers punishing themselves.

- The humanistic view is that we perfect ourselves by choosing what is right. This ignores our depravity. The positive confession teaching counsels people to *just say it*. However, we are not made holy merely because we profess it, claim it, or confess it to be so.

- Liberalism is inadequate because it rejects the concept that we have a sinful nature. In early history this was known once as Pelagianism. Our doctrine of salvation cannot rise above our doctrine of sin. If Jesus did not die to save us from ourselves, then, at best, his life is a great moral example which inspires us to live a holy life through our good works.

- The biblical doctrine of a holy life has also been obscured by the teaching that a holy life is possible only after death or that holiness is possible at the hour of death. Death is our enemy (1 Cor 15:26), not our friend. We can serve God in holiness and righteousness "all our days" (Luke 1:75). We can be preserved blameless until the coming of our Lord Jesus Christ (1 Thess 5:23). But the return of Christ will not remove sin since he already put away sin at his first appearing. He will bring final sanctification or glorification at his second advent. The promises and commands of Scripture imply that entire sanctification is possible before death and that the believer may be preserved in this condition culminating, not beginning with Christ's return.

- It has been taught that Romans 7 is the highest state of grace that the elect may enjoy in this life. However, the true Christian, regardless of his or her presuppositions, still has the Holy Spirit at work within who is striving to make them all that God wants to be. Once such Calvinist is famous for his prayer, "Lord, make me as holy as a pardoned sinner can be made." Thus, his hunger for a holy life trumped his doctrinal limitations.

- It has been asserted that regeneration and entire sanctification occur simultaneously. Wesley refuted this view.

1) There is such a thing as *perfection*; for it is again and again mentioned in Scripture.
2) It is not so early as justification; for justified persons are to "go on to perfection."
3) It is not so late as death; for St. Paul spake of living men that were perfect.

- It is widely taught that there is no deliverance from sin in this life. This is based on a dualistic view that anything physical is sinful, therefore the body is sinful and we will be sinful until we leave the body. Thus, any holiness, then, is positional or imputed. The obedience of Christ is imputed or reckoned to our account so that a person who is morally impure is accounted as holy. Our standing in Christ may be very different from our actual state.

- Evangelicalism tends to define a godly sorrow for sin as evidence of conversion. Thus, after baptized and received in to church membership, they are sometimes discipled about the deeper life or the higher life — two phrases which describe the same reality.

- If they are counseled to say that they have entered such a new level based on presumption which is presented as faith, nothing has really happened. They might not even be a Christian. Sadly, they are also often taught that they cannot lose it.

- If they do experience a new relationship with God, they may have experienced salvation but are counseled that they have received assurance, they have entered a new level, or that they are sanctified. The terminology depends primarily on whether the doctrinal bias is Keswick or holiness tradition.

- They could be told that now that they are a Christian they need to be baptized with the Holy Spirit. In holiness churches this is equated with sanctification. In Pentecostal churches this is evidenced by speaking in other tongues. In Pentecostal-holiness church this is the third work of grace. Eventually, however, physical manifestations become more important than holy living.

- Such personal quests for holiness tend to intersect with asceticism. Ascetic practice emphasizes discipline, but can end up as masochism — self-atonement for our sin. Monasticism was greatest organized quest for perfection in history. Sometimes these journeys overlap. The asceticism practiced in a monastery may differ only in degree from a holiness asceticism.

- "The techniques for obtaining entire sanctification sometimes received more attention than holiness itself." In legalistic circles the teaching is that we help God sanctify ourselves by doing things which are self-effacing. We are supposed to put the sinful nature to death by humiliating ourselves. This can become a Christless sanctification. In these circles the "mature" can sometimes be identified because they wear "holiness" uniforms. The irony is that they can keep their own organizational rules while at the same time be breaking God's law. Thus, they can be legalistic and lawless!

Wesley taught that we are sanctified by faith in the work of Christ and that faith is the only condition of sanctification. "I believe this perfection is always wrought in the soul by a simple act of faith."

- Those who become disillusioned with the institutional church tend to become mystics who embrace a vague spirituality in isolation. Terms like *mysticism* can be used in a derogatory sense without ever having defined them. Anyone who professes to have communion with God through Christ in prayer, a direct assurance from God regarding their salvation, and seeks to be led by his Spirit are usually labeled *mystic*. In its worst sense mysticism describes personal experience which is confirming only to the individual who experiences it and is not necessarily Christian. This strand runs through all world religions and can overlap with gnosticism.

- Monasticism has been called the greatest organized pursuit of perfection in history. Monasticism emphasized holiness through withdrawal from the world and vows of poverty, chastity, and discipline. "Such regulations indeed have an appearance of wisdom, with their self-imposed worship, their false humility and their harsh treatment of the body, but they lack any value in restraining sensual indulgence" (Col 2:23; Gal 3:3). In contrast, Wesley taught a social holiness. "The Gospel of Christ knows of no religion, but social; no holiness but social holiness." He advised, "It is a blessed thing to have fellow travelers to the New Jerusalem. If you cannot find any, you must make them; for none can travel that road alone."

- Supernatural manifestations such as tongues and miracles do not necessarily lead to a holy life (Matt 7:21-23). A leading Pentecostal scholar conceded that the baptism in the Holy Spirit, as they understand it, "is not of itself a sanctifying experience."

- Those who react against emotionalism tend to gravitate to more highly liturgical worship. They revel in the mystical beauty of symbols. They also glory in their ancient tradition. While God can meet them in high-church worship, the balance is between corporate worship and personal experience. While the sacraments are a means of grace, the symbols do not necessarily produce a holy life. Sacramentalism is a corporate view of perfection that believes the body is holy even if all its parts are unholy.

- A deeper life convention held annually in Keswick, England teaches the Holy Spirit counteracts the sin nature and helps us suppress it. We agree that this is our condition in regeneration (Gal 5:17-24), but we believe God's grace can take us beyond this condition.

- *Eradicate* means to pull up by the roots. The danger in using this term is that it conveys the concept that sin is a physical substance that can be removed once and for all, like a tooth is extracted or the roots of a tree dug out. This amounts to making something concrete out of an idea or abstraction.

- If the American holiness movement put too much emphasis on a crisis experience, their scholars today have put too much emphasis on process. It is not necessary to embrace process philosophy in order to understand that sanctification is both crisis and process. Although salvation is an ongoing process, however, there must be a first moment of actualization. If everything is process, there is no victory. Nothing is decisive. But justification and regeneration are instantaneous because they are sovereign works of God. Entire sanctification is also a sovereign free gift of grace. It is not accomplished by submission or consecration. And because it can only be realized through faith in the atonement of Christ, the cleansing can happen in a moment of time.

- All of these existential routes to spiritual perfection have caused some to put all their emphasis on objective truth. They trumpet the doctrine of imputed righteousness, regardless of how a person actually lives. In these circles one can be filled with the Spirit without ever knowing it. All that is necessary is the acceptance of certain propositional statements. The Christian life can become a one-time decision which produces no transformation.

- In liberation theology, personal piety is rejected and genuine salvation is reframed as liberation of the poor and oppressed. Thus, Vladimir Lenin is regarded as a serious source for theology and organized resistance to capitalism is the hallmark of Christian perfection.

While liberation theology is an attempt to baptize an atheistic position in Christian language, there is an element of truth in every other perspective. These various emphases are not necessarily contradictory. The will of God is reflected in a consensus of these views.

What Next?

According to Hebrews 12:14 holiness is both a right relationship with God and with mankind. We are commanded to pursue this kind of right relationship. Most evangelicals are not motivated to seek holiness because they have been taught that they are sinners saved by grace and that is all they can ever be. However, those who have been truly awakened are not content to wallow in sin.

The command to seek holiness (Heb 12:14) is still applicable to those who are growing in holiness. While we must wait upon God to do the work, we do not wait passively, but attend to all the means of grace. Sanctification is made possible by God's grace, yet we must exercise a present-tense obedient faith.

As we walk in light, the blood cleanses (1 John 1:7). We are to attend to the means of grace: prayer and fasting, daily Bible reading and reading of devotional literature, spiritual conversation, public worship and the sacraments, be accountable to a small group, and giving financially. We will grow spiritually as we learn spiritual discipline. But while all this will weaken sin, it will not drive it out. God alone can cleanse us.

Yet there is little seeking after holiness today within any theological camp. But this holiness hunger is a mark of the genuine work of the Holy Spirit — whether in preliminary grace, justifying grace, or perfecting grace.

The Bible teaches that obedient believers will become increasingly convicted of the nature of sin still remaining in them. As they walk in the Spirit, they will be led to a full cleansing from the inner nature of sin and filled with a holy love toward God and our neighbor through the sanctifying work of the Holy Spirit. This work is begun in a moment and is ongoing.

This sanctification, resulting in Christian perfection, implies neither the end of growth or progress, nor absolute perfection. It is a relative perfection in which God imparts holiness and imputes perfection to those who are governed by and who continue to develop in his holy love.

May God help you understand his purpose for you and where you are in the process. There are many extremes and excesses to avoid. If you are bound by sin, the Holy Spirit will make you miserable until you cry out for help. When you trust in the atoning work of Christ on the cross, he will forgive your sins and give you the Holy Spirit. The Holy Spirit will begin the process of making you Christlike. As you walk in the Spirit, he will do everything he has promised and commanded. If it is ever received at all, it is received by a simple act of faith. Thus, we should expect it every moment.

For complete exegesis, historical development, theological positions, and documentation, see Vic Reasoner, *A Wesleyan Theology of Holy Living for the Twenty-first Century: The Pursuit of Perfection Across Twenty Centuries*. Evansville, IN: Fundamental Wesleyan Publishers, 2012. 2 vols. 928 pages. ISBN 978-0-9761003-2-4

www.ingramcontent.com/pod-product-compliance
Lightning Source LLC
Chambersburg PA
CBHW070043070426
42449CB00012BA/3151